On the legal procedure of the Anglo-Saxons : communitcated to the Society of antiquaries

Henry Charles Coote

ON

THE LEGAL PROCEDURE

OF THE

ANGLO-SAXONS.

COMMUNICATED TO THE SOCIETY OF ANTIQUARIES

BY

HENRY CHARLES COOTE, ESQ., F.S.A.

LONDON

J B NICHOLS AND SONS, PRINTERS, 25, PARLIAMENT STREET

1867.

FROM

THE ARCHÆOLOGIA,

Vol XLI

ON THE

LEGAL PROCEDURE OF THE ANGLO-SAXONS.

THE Anglo-Saxon legal procedure has failed to attract the attention either of the antiquary or the lawyer. The causes of this neglect, however, do not readily suggest themselves. As a practice it must have had merit, for amongst other germs which fructified under the fosterage of the Norman we find in it that of the English jury in a state of inception prompt for further development. With such bearings upon the future, this legal procedure may, I think, be reasonably regarded as a subject worthy of antiquarian research.

The Anglo-Saxon law discriminated its legal practice according as the object of the proceeding was reparation to an individual or vindication of the public interest. In other words, as it recognised civil suits and criminal prosecutions, so it varied its procedure in relation to each.

Of the Anglo-Saxon civil suit, the incidents were such as inspired confidence in a suitor whether he sought to protect a right or to assert it. The system must therefore have been settled and unswerving, such as a weak man could appeal to, and a powerful man could not override. Nothing can more forcibly illustrate the consistency of the system, and the confidence which it inspired, than a record which Mr Kemble has edited in his great compilation.

King Æthelred, having satisfied himself by an extra-judicial inquiry, conducted in his own way, that certain lands at Hæcceburn and at Bradanfeld, though occupied by one Leofwin, belonged of right to one Wynflæd, "sent straightway to Leofwin and signified this to him. Then would he not unless it was shot (referred) to the County Court (scirgemot). Then did man so;" and the cause was tried at the County Court after the usual manner of civil actions.[*]

We may regard this record as proving two things—that the right of a freeman to have his matters adjudicated in the Court of his county could not be superseded

---

[*] Cod. Diplom vol. iii p 292

a

by the interposition of authority; that the confidence which a defendant could feel in the method of that Court, though his antagonist were supported by the *magnates* of the nation, could only have been inspired by a knowledge that its proceedings were consistent and regular.

That being the character of the procedure, it should not be difficult, and it may be curious, to resuscitate its legal order.

In the first place, it would seem that an application of some sort was made by a plaintiff to some person having authority in connexion with the shire and its judicature. It is not, however, quite clear what this preliminary step was

It may have been an application to the ealdorman sitting amongst the assembled county judges,[a] or it may have been made to the sheriff out of Court.

The immediate consequence of this step was the granting to the plaintiff of a summons against the defendant.[b] In the words of the Anglo-Saxon law, the latter was mooted to a County Court to attend on some day during the ordinary sittings of the scyrgemot, or at a Court specially appointed.[c]

The plaintiff equally with the defendant received a summons to attend the Court[d]

On the day appointed, both suitors, if obedient to the summons, attended the Court. They brought with them their several witnesses, and the trial took place.

Such a trial (one of ejectment) has been *resumé* by an Anglo-Saxon lawyer in these words :[e]

"Calumniam explicuerunt, et causam ventilaverunt ac discusserunt; cognitáque rei veritate, per judicium abstulerunt Bluntesham a filiis Bogan pro duabus causis"

---

[a] See the expression in Ine's Laws, c. 8 (Ancient Laws and Institutes published by the Record Commission)

[b] In the laws of Hlothhære and Eadric (c 8) it is said, "If a man make plaint against another in a suit, and he cite (moot) the man to a methel or a thing," &c. (Gif man óðerne sace tihte, and he ðane mannan mote an meðle oþþe an þinge) Here the plaint precedes the citation or summons. In the Book of Ely (p. 150 of edit. London, 1848), Brihtnoth the ealdorman orders a defendant to be summoned (jussit summoneri). These two passages being read together support the assertion in the text

[c] Besides the ordinary sittings of the County Court, which were five in number, three being held in cities and two in the country, the ealdorman could appoint as many others as should be necessary (Cnut's Laws, Secular, c 18, buton hit oftor neod si)

[d] Book of Ely, (ed Stewart) p 139 "Nec mora, fit maxima concio, summonetur Wlnothus (defendant) ad placitum, summonentur et filii Bogan (plaintiffs)." See p 138, ibid

[e] Book of Ely (ibidem) I attribute the expression to an Anglo-Saxon lawyer advisedly. The writer, who in this chronicle describes Anglo-Saxon law-suits, shows the technical knowledge of a lawyer, and by his use of Anglo-Saxon inflections must have been an Anglo-Saxon, and not an Englishman writing *post Conquestum*

In the concrete no modern could describe a trial at the assizes in words more satisfactory to those who care less for details than results.

To those who do not, I will endeavour to extend the summary into its Anglo-Saxon particulars.

As the first thing of all, the plaintiff was called upon by the judges to make his claim (geagnian).[a]

This was initiated by his taking an oath describing his claim and averring that it was just and well founded [b]

This was the plaintiff's fore-oath, a step which could never be dispensed with.[c]

If the plaintiff would not give it, judgment went for the defendant.[d]

After this was done the plaintiff "led" his witnesses.[e]

Attention is due to this word, for it expresses the voluntary attendance of witnesses upon a plaintiff, that which in Anglo-Norman law was afterwards called suit or suite.

This leading was peculiar to the civil action.

The witnesses so led by the plaintiff attended out of clanship, or perhaps the sense of justice and duty.

Their attendance was enforced by no legal compulsion; they were not subpœnaed and did not appear to a call. In a civil suit there existed no legal means of enforcing the attendance of witnesses either in the interest of plaintiff or defendant.

And, as it was in the power of these witnesses to stay away or refuse their attendance when and as they pleased, the trial of an Anglo-Saxon action was often deferred over a space of years.[f]

This ultroneous character of the witnesses should be noted, as it is the great and leading distinction between the evidence in civil and in criminal cases.

The plaintiff's witnesses on their production all in turn took the following oath :

---

[a] Cod. Dipl vol iii p 292   "Then man assigned Wynflæd that she must *geahnian*," &c.

[b] Ibid and Cnut's Laws, Secular, cc 22

[c] Cnut, *as above*.

[d] Book of Ely, p 139. " Sed filii Bogan (plaintiffs) noluerunt suscipere juramentum, statuerunt itaque omnes ut Wlnothus Bluntesham haberet "

[e] Book of Ely, pp. 130, 139, " produxit, adduxit," Cod Dipl *as above*, Wynflæd "led the ahnung," Confessionale Ecgberti, c. 34, " Se ðe bið on aðe gelædd," &c.

[f] Book of Ely, p. 141, " Qua de causa lis et altercatio permaxima orta est, et multos annos habita, inter eos ," and (*ibid*) " res etenim eadem multis annis in lite versabatur "

" In the name of the Almighty God, as I here for N. in true witness stand un-bidden and unbought, so I with my eyes oversaw, and with my ears overheard, that which I with him say."[a]

If this oath be not sufficient to show that the witnesses gave testimony in a civil suit in the sense in which we now understand that term, we learn from another source that they did so; that they afforded details at the same time that they directly verified the fact or transaction in question.[b]

It appears that a definite number of consentient witnesses was necessary to prove the plaintiff's case. If this definite number gave a consensual testimony, in the words of the Anglo-Saxon law the plaintiff gave the full oath.[c]

It may be fairly supposed, however, that the number varied with the nature and character of the suit, the vindication of a strayed cow would not demand an equal number with the claim for a manor and its royalties. And witnesses would be more numerous in civil cases than in criminal, as the issue of the latter would be more narrowed.

If the full oath was not given, the plaintiff was non-suited.[d]

If on the contrary it was given in its fulness, it then became incumbent upon the defendant to make out his defence if he had one •

If he had no defence, that is, if he would not consent to take the fore-oath which I shall presently mention, and which was the prelude to his evidence, the plaintiff was entitled to judgment.[f]

---

[a] See oaths in Thorpe's Laws   Also Cnut's Laws, Secular, c 23

[b] Book of Ely, p 150.   The ealdorman " veniens ad Dittune, cœpit ibi disserere et enarrare causas et calumpnias, conventiones, et pacta infracta, quæ habuit super eum, per testimonium multorum legalium hominum "   See also a clearer instance at p 130, ' producti ergo testes . . . perhibuerunt testimonium, &c   Then follow details of evidence.

[c] Cod Dipl vol iii p 293   " Then she led the ahnung, &c   until all the full oath were forth come both in men and women '   Book of Ely, p. 139   " Wlnothus adduxit secum illuc perplures viros fideles, scilicet omnes meliores de vi hundredis .   Tunc Wlnothus adduxit fideles viros plusquam mille ut per juramentum illorum sibi vindicarent eandem terram."   Wlnothus was defendant.

[d] This may be inferred from the fact of the law requiring the full oath to be adduced by the plaintiff.

[e] See the Cod Dipl as above.   Here the plaintiff had taken the fore-oath, and had led up the full number of witnesses, who swore with her.   " Then quoth the witan, who were there, that it were better that man let (the defendant's) oath away than that man should give it, because thereafter there would be no friendship," &c   The judgment of the Court was that the land should be restored to the plaintiff

[f] Cod Dipl. as above   Book of Ely, p 150   " Cui, omnia illata deneganti et contradicenti, statuerunt ut cum jure jurando se purgaret, quod cum facere nequibat, nec, qui secum jurare debuerant, habere poterat, decretum est, ut eo expulso Brihtnothus alderman utrisque hydis uteretur."

If the defendant had a defence he proceeded as follows:

The defendant took his fore-oath, deposing to his innocent possession or his lawful purchase of the chose in question, that the goods sold were sound, that the debt was paid, &c.[a] He then led or produced his witnesses, who took an oath similar to that of the plaintiff's witnesses

These witnesses were as voluntary as those of the plaintiff.

If the defendant's witnesses gave consensual evidence on the oath, some fixed number constituting a full oath, but which does not appear, the plaintiff's claim would be contradicted, and the defendant would be dismissed.[b]

If this consensual evidence of the defendant broke down, i e if the full oath on his part was not given, the plaintiff was entitled to judgment, and obtained it of the Court.[c]

From what I have stated in regard to Anglo-Saxon civil procedure, the reader will have seen that it is identical with what in succeeding generations was called in England the wager of law.

After judgment followed execution, unless the plaintiff consented to take security in lieu of immediate execution.[d]

In the criminal prosecution the proceeding was as follows:

The delinquent was accused (probably at a County Court) by some person who *pro eâ vice* constituted himself prosecutor.[e]

The accused was at liberty to give security to appear and take his trial if he could provide it, and the security might be given upon his own property or be that of bail. Otherwise he was consigned to a King's prison until the day of trial.[f]

---

[a] See oaths in the Laws.

[b] This is to be inferred, as without it there could be no defence. It is supported by the analogy of the function of the other oath—the criminal oath If the accused's witnesses all swore consentiently, the accused was acquitted If they did not so do, the oath burst, and the accused was convicted See Æthelred's Domas, c. 1.

[c] Book of Ely *passim*

[d] Hlothhære and Eadric's Laws, c 10; Book of Ely, p. 137 "Tunc judicantes statuerunt, ut abbas suam terram cum palude et piscatione habere deberet, statuerunt etiam ut Begmundus et cognati præfatæ viduæ suum piscem de vi annis abbati solverent et regi forisfacturam darent, statuerunt quoque ut si sponte sua hoc reddere nollent, captione suæ pecuniæ constricti justificarentur." See an instance of the County Court Judges assessing damages in their judgment in the Book of Ely, p 128

[e] Ine's Laws, c 62 Ælfred's Laws, c 22 The latter has reference to a criminal prosecution See the use of the word "yppe" in Pœnitentiali Ecgberti, additam c. 2.

[f] Ine's Laws, c. 62.

On that day he appeared in discharge of his bail, or was brought up by the custodian of the gaol.

The Court being assembled, the prosecutor took a fore-oath of the following tenor :[a]

" By the Lord I accuse not N either for hatred or for envy, or for unlawful lust of gain, nor know I anything soother; but as my informant to me said, and I myself in sooth believe, that he was the thief of my property."

The crime would of course vary.

This fore-oath was indispensable, and gave to the accusation (tihtl) its legal effect[b]

When the prosecutor had taken the oath, the accused was bound to clear himself " if he dared."[c]

The trial from this period became the " lad " or clearing of the accused.[d]

The order of his purgation was as follows:

He took an oath, in assertion of his own innocence, of this tenor :[e]

" By the Lord I am guiltless both in deed and counsel of the accusation (tihtl) which N charges against me."

This was the preliminary of the " lad."[f]

The fore-oath of the accused had therefore the effect of a pleader of Not Guilty, and upon this issue the evidence was gone into

Without it, *i.e.* if the accused dared not take it, there could be and was no trial, for there was no innocence to assert, the accused being considered guilty, because he had rejected the means which the law allowed him of asserting his innocence.

I have said that the accused was bound by law to clear himself of the charge.

This neither in fact nor in theory amounted to the same thing as the throwing upon him the *onus* of proving his own innocence, for by the manner in which the evidence was collected and obtained the result of the trial was practically the same as if the *onus probandi* lay upon the prosecutor.

The marshalling and taking of the evidence was thus conducted:

There was only one set of witnesses in a criminal matter, and this was in general parlance called the " lad," as the clearing of the accused depended upon the result of its opinion.[g]

[a] See oaths in Laws.　　　　　　　　　　　　　　[b] Ordinance respecting the Dunsætas, c. 6.

[c] Ælfred and Guthrum's Peace, c 3, " gif he hine ladian dyrre "

[d] The Laws, *passim.*　　　　　　　[e] See oath in Laws　　　　　　[f] Ine, c. 54

[g] Ine, c 54, Dunsætas, c. 6; Æthelred's Domas, c 13.

accused.

They were not voluntary. On the contrary, their attendance in Court was wholly compulsory, for they were *named, i.e.* nominated and subpœnaed, by the sheriff of the county,[a] that officer being in these ages the vice-judge of the county.

They were summoned by that officer from the hundred where the *corpus delicti* lay, *i. e.* the venue or vicinity.[b]

The witnesses so summoned were the equals or peers of the accused.[c]

A larger number of witnesses was named than was afterwards actually sworn.[d]

Where witnesses were thus forced upon the accused, it would be only fair that there should be some power in him of obtaining their rejection should they be provably uncreditable, hostile, or malignant.

This safeguard against injustice the Anglo-Saxons possessed.[e]

The accused might choose his witnesses, to the extent of a defined number, out of the gross number summoned, and the choice of these witnesses was the rejection of the rest.

The selected witnesses were denominated the cyreath.[f]

The witnesses were then sworn in the following formula, that is, if they could consent, all or in major part, to take it.[g]

The oath was this :

" By the Lord the oath is clean and unperjured which N. (the accused) has sworn."

It would seem probable that a majority of the oath found the verdict, for as they were witnesses nothing more was required than a weight of evidence

If the whole or the majority took this oath, the accused was acquitted.[h]   If

---

[a] Æthelred's Domas, c. 13, Æthelstan's Laws, c. 9, Laws of the Northumbrian Priests, cc 51, 52, 53.

[b] Hlothhære and Eadric, c 5   This is a direct authority, but the general rule of law is also inferrible from the sub-rule that where the accused was *infamis* the oath was to be summoned out of several hundreds Cnut's Laws, c 22

[c] Ine's Laws, c 30, " by his own were " But this is stated more explicitly in the Laws of the Northumbrian Priests, cc. 51, 52, 53, and Wihtræd, c 21. Ælfred and Guthrum's Peace, c. 3

[d] See *post*

[e] " Odium vel aliquid competens " Hen. I L L c 31, § 8 , Æthelstan, c. 10. (Perjury.)

[f] Dunsætas c 6   Cnut, c. 66   See also LL Hen I. c. 31, s. 6, 7, 8   These sections refer to the jury.

[g] See oaths in Laws, Thorpe, vol 1 p. 181. The position of this oath, as following those of the prosecutor and the accused, shows it to be that of the jury.

[h] Æthelred's Domas, c. 13

they declined taking the oath wholly or in part, the oath burst, and the accused was convicted   the lad failed [a]

The witnesses in a criminal prosecution did not give evidence, but were limited to the form of oath I have quoted.

The rationale of this is evident . the Court had taken measures to summon those who were best acquainted with the fact in question.   And whatever opinion they solemnly found was accepted by the Court without criticism.

The result of the swearing, whether it showed the consensual opinion of all or of a majority, was held to carry conviction of the fact, and to bind the Court, with whom there rested no discretion except to believe it.[b]

Upon the foundation of this finding of the witnesses, the judges made their decree and all such subsidiary orders as might be necessary.

In all this there is much to approve of   Though the Anglo-Saxons could leave the evidence of civil matters to the parties interested in the result, they saw and enforced a distinction between those suits and criminal matters.   They made provision that the witnesses in the latter case should be compulsory, in order that no evidence should be lost, and that the witnesses should not be tampered with by either side; above all, that they should come from the venue, the place where the offence was committed, and where its proofs lay.   And with this there was freedom left to the accused, which enabled him to weed away those who hated him or unduly favoured the prosecutor.

All this however is totally beyond the capacity of the mere Anglo-Saxon; I mean his capacity for original conception and invention.

The principles must therefore mount higher than the incoming of this nation; and it is in the history of our country that we shall find the solution.

The historical source to which I refer both the civil and the criminal procedure, of the Anglo-Saxons is Roman, the law of this country before the Anglo-Saxons effected their settlements.[c]

The procedure of a civil suit, *judicium privatum,* according to the Roman law as it existed in Western Europe may be stated thus

[a] Eadward, c 3, Dunsætas, cc 4 and 6   The latter authority regards the oath as being *torn,* but the metaphor is not very dissimilar.

[b] Wihtræd, c 21, Domas of Æthelred, c 13   The first authority declares the verdict to be uncontrovertible, the other that the "doom" of the jury shall stand.

[c] This assertion is very much strengthened by the interesting fact that the jury, as the Anglo-Saxons understood it, is to be found in the early Welsh Laws

There were issuable pleadings resembling in effect those which our own legal practice has made familiar to us.

The evidence in support of the issues was entirely voluntary on the part of the witnesses both of the plaintiff and of the defendant.[a] Until the reform of Justinian the subpœna did not exist in civil cases [b]

This was the great distinction between evidence as taken in a civil suit, and as taken in a criminal prosecution.

As regards the preliminary steps of the latter before the taking of the evidence the following is a summary.

Bail was accepted for the appearance of the accused.[c]

The accuser made a formal and detailed accusation, which he either presented in writing at the bureau of the *Præses* or it was taken down *apud acta* at the same place by some official [d]

In other cases, as of public robbers, the *irenarchæ* arrested them and sent them to trial.

After this had been done, the accused, according to the nature of the charge or his own position in society, was sent to prison, committed to the safe keeping of a guard, was admitted to bail or was relieved from giving it.[e]

The principles by which a criminal trial was regulated were these.

The accused was bound to prove his *intention,* as the effect of his charge was called.[f]

So far he was like a plaintiff, but with the fear of a *talio* in addition [g]

But by the same law also the accused was bound to purge himself; "*purgare se debet,*" says Ulpian.[h]

The first of these principles is of course plain and plausible enough, but the other as a rule of law, in respect of its seeming injustice, requires some explana-

---

[a] Cod 4, tit 20, de Testibus, s. 16, Novell de Test 90 c 8.

[b] Accordingly great facilities were afforded for giving evidence in civil matters   The judge who tried the cause might take the evidence orally or he might read at the trial evidence taken elsewhere, the latter consisting of depositions or voluntary affidavits made before any *magistratus* within whose provinces or territories the witnesses might be   Cod 4, 20, pp 2, 15, and 20, ibid tit 21, p, 18   See the expressions used in Dig 22 tit. 5, p 3, § 4, and p 22   See also Quinctilian, Instit Orat 5, 7.

[c] See Calvin's Lex Jurid and Festus *sub voce Vadem*

[d] Paulus in Dig. 48, tit 2, cc 3 and 6, ibid tit 5, c. 11, p 6, Cod. 9, tit. 2, c 8.

[e] Dig 48, tit. 3, c. 1, and the following *capita*

[f] Dig. 48, tit. 18, c 18, p 2   [g] Symmachi Epist lib 10, ep ult.

[h] See the expression repeated, Dig 48, tit. 1. c. 5, ibid. tit 4, c 11, ibid tit 17, c 1, p 3, c 5. So Apuleius, de Mundo, c. 35, " Reus purgandi se necessitate, insectandi studio accusator venit "

tion. Its injustice, however, had more of seeming than of reality. And it would appear after all to have been only a *façon de parler*, for other authorities show that its real and operative meaning was no more or less than this,—the *reus* should leave it to the proofs of the case to show his innocence [a]

This being so, there must have been something in the mode of inquiry to make it possible, and so there was

A Roman criminal trial was a public inquest conducted by the magistrate who presided over the country where the crime was committed.[b]

The law called it emphatically an investigation of the truth.[c]

This great local judge ordered all such witnesses to appear as the accuser vouched (laudavit), and as he himself thought necessary.[d] In other words, they were subpœnaed.

And as these were days of limited locomotion, all the necessary witnesses would be within the summoning power of the judge

Every person who could be alleged to be *cognitor vel præsens* was subpœnaed.[e]

The evocation of the witnesses by the Court rendered them only one set. This is contrasted with the production of witnesses on each side in a civil suit [f]

Witnesses in criminal cases were always confronted with the judge [g]

Witnesses being gathered together by these means, it would frequently happen that they knew nothing of the matter upon which they had been summoned

The Roman law provided for this. The witness being sworn to give his testimony of what he knew, might swear that he knew nothing [h]

[a] That the Roman system rendered the truth attainable we are assured by a Roman subject and citizen Apuleius (De Magia) says, " Quippe insimulari quivis innocens potest, revinci nisi nocens non potest."

[b] *Passim* in the Laws St Cyprian, Epist 54 " Cum statutum sit ab omnibus nobis . . ut unus cujusque causa illic audiatur, ubi est crimen admissum "

[c] Cod. 9, tit 41, c 8

[d] Cod Theod 11, tit 39, c 13; and Godefroye's learned and interesting note, Cod. 4, c 20, pp 11, 16, Novell, 90, p 8, Symmach, *ante* For an exception to the rule see Pliny's Letters, lib. 5, ep. 20, see also Domat (Strahan's translation), vol 1 p 451 Dr Smith is thus wrong in stating generally that there was no subpœna before Justinian (Classical Dictionary, p. 529)

[e] See the expressions used by the Council of Carthage quoted by Godefroye in his note to Cod Theod 11, tit 39, c 8, " in judicium ad testimonium devocari eum quia cognitor vel præsens fuerit "

[f] Cod 4, tit. 20, p 11 That the evidence taken at a criminal trial was considered one context only— the result of the judicial inquiry —appears by the expressions of Constantine (Cod Theod 11, tit. 36, c 1) " Quod si reus . . partem, pro defensione sui ex testibus quæstioneque propositâ, possit arripere parte vero obrui, accusarique videatur,' &c

[g] Dig 48, tit 18, c 1, p 21, Cod 4, tit 20, p 14, " ad judicantis intrare secretum "

[h] Justinian's recital in Cod. 4, tit 20, p 16

The Roman law affected a number of witnesses.[a]

One witness, whatever his position, was not allowed even to be heard.[b]

The number varied with the cause.

Sometimes there should be three, sometimes five [c]

But whatever the required number might be it was essential to the case set up, and without it the case failed

The accused was allowed the privilege of obtaining the rejection of a witness by showing a just exception against him, e. g. that he was *publico judicio damnatus*, bribed, infamous in character, or the like.[d]

If such an exception was proved, the witness was not called

The law required that the conviction should be upon the agreement of the witnesses. Constantine says, "Omnium qui tormentis vel interrogationibus fuerunt dediti, in unum conspirantem concordantemque rei fine convictus sit et sic in objecto flagitio deprehensus, ut vix jam ipse, ea quæ commiserit negare sufficiat "[e]

The proof adduced before the judge instructed his conscience. "Si nulla probatio religionem cognoscentis instruat," says a legal authority [f]

Still he was free to use his judgment conscientiously: "Verumtamen quod legibus omissum est, non omittetur religione judicantium, ad quorum officium pertinet, ejus quoque testimonii fidem, quod integræ frontis homo dixerit perpendere," says another great authority [g]

In both the procedures, the civil and the public, there were preliminary oaths taken by each side, the plaintiff and defendant, the prosecutor and accused.

In the civil suit it would seem to have been optional for the plaintiff to put the defendant to his oath. But if he did so, he in turn was compelled to take the oath of calumny

In the criminal proceding the prosecutor was obliged by law to take the oath in all cases [h]

I think that the aforegoing evidences will identify the Anglo-Saxon procedure,

[a] Dig 22, tit. 5, p 1, § 2, ibid p 12, p 3, § 2

[b] Cod 4, tit 20, p 9

[c] Cod. 4, c. 20, p 15

[d] Dig 22, tit 5, p 3, § 5   [e] Cod Theod 9, tit. 40, c 1

[f] Dig 48, tit 18, c 1, pp 17

[g] Dig. 22, tit 5, c 13.

[h] Domat, vol i p 452 (Strahan's translation), and Dr Smith's Dictionary   See also Dig 12, tit 2,

p 34

civil and criminal, with the Roman, and in so doing will show that the Anglo-Saxon criminal oath was a transmission of Roman law

If this be so, it only remains to show that the Anglo-Saxon oath, which was the same as the Anglo-Norman,* contained the germ of the later English jury.

The points of identity are these :

The Anglo-Saxon oath is the venue, that is, the persons who are to give it come from the vicinity of the crime and the criminal, and for that reason should know the whole truth of the matter. This would be particularly the case in ages when locomotion was always difficult and sometimes prohibited.

They are the peers, of the accused.

They are compulsorily summoned by the sheriff.

They swear to a result.

This result determines the fact at issue, binds the Court, and must be accepted by them

These substantial resemblances being coexistent in each, there only remained for the Anglo-Saxon oath one point of development, and the jury, as we understand it, would rise into legal existence. The oath should lose its obligation of giving testimony, exchanging it for the privilege of expressing its collective view upon the fact at issue

This could not be accomplished until witnesses were produced and examined before the persons who composed the oath. When that was done the English jury was created. Still establishers of fact as before, they thenceforth exercised their function judicially, not as privileged witnesses having a prerogative of testimony.

When this change occurred is not precisely known.

We only know clearly to whom that change is due.

The acute Norman, with the finest legal mind since the days of the Empire, had seen some, though possibly not all, of the advantages concealed under the " lad," and from a purgation converted it into a trial

To him we are indebted as well for the word as for the development of the proceeding.

* See Liber Albus (Riley's edition), pp 56, 57, 58

\

CPSIA information can be obtained at www.ICGtesting.com
Printed in the USA
LVOW111718090912

298041LV00015B/198/P